Ecosystems

The Network of Life!

Om
KIDZ
An imprint of Om Books International

It was a beautiful Sunday morning. Jane and Judy were standing by their bedroom window.

Suddenly, Jane exclaimed, "Look Judy! There is a small mound of sand in the middle of our garden. Where did that come from?"

"It's an anthill. Ants live underground. They make colonies by digging up sand," Judy explained.

"I don't like ants. They crawl around everywhere and even bite. Why do they even exist?" Jane shuddered, thinking about the time when ants had crawled up inside her dress and bitten her.

"Ants, like all other living creatures, are an important part of the ecosystem," explained Judy.

"What is an 'ecosystem', Judy?" Jane asked.

"The plants and animals as well as non-living things that are found in a particular area are referred to as an 'ecosystem'. The plants and animals present in an ecosystem are dependent on each other, as well as on their environment for survival. Every ecosystem is based on a very delicate balance. Even the slightest disturbance would affect all the creatures that are a part of it," Judy explained.

"Can you tell me more about ecosystems?" asked Jane.

"There are several types of ecosystems. Some ecosystems exist in a small area such as the ant colonies underneath a rock, a decaying tree trunk, or a pond in your town. Some ecosystems exist in large forms such as a forest or lake. Amazingly, the Earth can be called a huge ecosystem. Do you remember our camping trip last summer?" Judy asked.

"Yes!" Jane replied with a smile.

They had set up a tent in the forest and had so much fun on that trip. A forest is also an ecosystem. It is a large area of land that has a variety of trees, plants and animals.

Forests that have warm temperatures and receive a lot of rainfall have a variety of plants and animals. Forests that are located in the cold and dry regions have less diversity.

"I remember that there were mountains behind the forest. They looked so huge!" Jane chimed in.

"Yes. The mountain ecosystem is barren and rocky with very high peaks. The climate changes according to the height of the mountain, so plants and animals have to adapt to the decreasing temperatures. The plants found in this ecosystem include shrubs, short grasses, mosses and lichens."

"Are there any other types of ecosystems?" Jane questioned.

"Yes!" Judy replied. "We also have the desert ecosystem which experiences extreme temperature changes. Plants such as the cactus are found here. They have thick leaves in order to ensure that there is minimum loss of water for the plant. Animals such as camels that live in deserts have 'humps' to store food for long periods of time."

"Are oceans and seas also a type of ecosystem?"

"Yes. The marine ecosystem is the biggest ecosystem in the world! It covers about 71% of Earth. It includes the five main oceans: the Pacific Ocean, Atlantic Ocean, Indian Ocean, Arctic Ocean and Southern Ocean, as well as many smaller gulfs and bays. Millions of varieties of fish, marine animals, insects and plants are found underwater," replied Judy.

"Judy, how do ecosystems maintain a balance?" asked curious little Jane.

"The plants and animals in an ecosystem are connected to each other through 'food chains'. Food chains help in maintaining the balance of an ecosystem. Plants form the first level of every food chain. They are known as producers as they produce their own food with the help of sunlight. Animals

and human beings who eat these plants are known as the primary consumers. Animals that eat other animals become the secondary consumers."

"Earthworms are called decomposers, as they eat the bodies of dead creatures."

"How will an imbalance in the ecosystem affect all the living creatures?" asked Jane.

"Human activities have resulted in a lot of environmental pollution. People are polluting land, water and air by dumping waste. Smoke from factories and vehicles are causing global warming. Forests are being cut to make farmlands and cities, forcing animals out of their homes. These activities disturb the balance of the ecosystems."

"Since all living creatures are connected to each other, they will all be affected by this imbalance!"

Jane was shocked to hear this. "Oh! I don't want the ecosystem to be destroyed. Is there any way that we can help conserve the ecosystem?"

Judy smiled and said, "We can contribute to the conservation of the environment in several ways, such as by planting more trees, using environment-friendly modes of transport and ensuring proper disposal of waste!"

"Let's do our bit too, by planting a tree," said Jane, enthusiastically. And together, the two sisters planted a sapling in the garden while enjoying the beautiful spring morning.